Poems of the Deepwoods Nitwit! and Tales of Way Back When

To Carol & Marshall

enjoy

Ethel Crownover

Poems of the Deepwoods Nitwit! and Tales of Way Back When

Ethel Crownover

Writers Club Press
San Jose New York Lincoln Shanghai

Poems of the Deepwoods Nitwit! and Tales of Way Back When

Writers Club Press
an imprint of iUniverse.com, Inc.

For information address:
iUniverse.com, Inc.
620 North 48th Street, Suite 201
Lincoln, NE 68504-3467
www.iuniverse.com

ISBN: 0-595-14458-6

Printed in the United States of America

To my brother, Taylor, who taught me to read and the love for books, with many happy hours of stories and tales of our family, and to accept the world in which we live that was changing so swiftly.

Foreword

Only in poetry can the best feelings be revealed and few words express so much. In poetry she's opened what in troubled hearts is sealed and in few words the hardest hearts touched. Her own life struck down by the loss of three sons has risen to proclaim in these simple words. While the frivolous masses make laughter and puns to mimic and tease cattle-like herds. She gives us insight into fortune and grief, we have both by our choice in her view. This wise lady explains all our problems in a manner so brief, but the many won't listen—only the few. Her wisdom is shown in the poems she's penned, her few words expressing so much. That wisdom we need in our hope to amend, what's wrong is found in her touch.

These things we find in the thoughts she has scribed, and left for those seeing to see. That life is a choice of the true and the tried, or a failure for you and for me. As Ethel's her name and friendship her fame, and logic and reason her goal, The mountains her footstool and it's people her game, and outsiders furnish her toll. Form the mountains she's bred, from it's wisdom she's filled, no better there is to be found.Our mind is her soil and our minds she has tilled, the better to give us firm ground. And to make us laugh, albeit at ourselves, Oft times she brings us some mirth. In a manner sweet as honey, or acid as lime, but always just what it's worth. This lady so wise and filled with true love, is truly a lady of lore. Her faith is in people created in the likeness above, of her wisdom and words we need more. But her heart is worn thin and her mind filled with doubt, no fault of her own can we see.

And she shouldn't be burdened by problems without clout, to correct them for you and for me. All her efforts for others, for family and friend—she has not a selfish bone. She tries and is true and faithful to the end, nothing wrong or hurt will she condone.

She knows the fun of laughter and play, her childhood was filled with glee. They barely had money to get by each day, but love and family was life to her key. So she's written so wise and she hopes we'll take note, her words are made to inspire. We need to take heed, and study what she wrote, and abide before we expire.

By James A. Woods

Preface

———— ∞ ————

AUTHORS NOTE

The poetry within the pages of this book are taken from the life, which though simple, was full of love, sorrow, and tragedy. Problems that were met head on, with a smile, and an expectation of something better tomorrow. My life, and my friends lives, I tried to fill with cheer through the crazy rhymes I jotted down at work, at home, and when I awakened at night with a thought running through my head. Each poem is from some part of the life I lived. Each morning my life started anew. Yesterday was gone forever, tomorrow was not yet and today was all I had to think about. Life in a time of a slower pace. A wonderful, beautiful life in another world, that can never be again. It should bring joy and tears to the elderly. To the young, laughter and wonder of what my world was all about.

Acknowledgments

---∞---

I wish to acknowledge the many friends who encouraged me to write this book. To all of you I traveled with, may you by chance find it tucked away and remember it was from my life and from those of you that inspired many of the poems. To my friends who put it all together for me and kept giving me that push I needed to get it published. To the elderly, may it bring happy memories of your youth. To the young, may it bring you closer to your roots and the desire to know of a time gone forever.

Introduction

---∞---

Within the pages of this book,
If by chance you dare to look.
You'll find time, as it used to be,
In the foothills and coves of Tennessee.

Tales from Grandpa, way back when,
Women were women, and men were men.
It was so simple, that wonderful life,
With a house full of kids, and a loving wife.

Poetry so different from any you've read,
From thoughts that were rushing through my head.
Life in good times, and life in the bad,
When we were happy and when we were sad.

A wonderful life when time stood still,
When a gorgeous sunset gave you a thrill.
When water was pure and air so sweet,
And fresh plowed ground warmed your bare feet.

This was a time in a much better world,
A time when I was a slip of a girl.
Would that I could go over this life again,
Each day I'd greet gladly like I did back then.

CHILDHOOD MEMORIES

I built my playhouse in the rocks,
Beside the mountain high.
And there I kept my little house,
Beneath the blue, blue sky.
My dishes were the broken bits,
Of china from a far off land.
And on the rock, that was my stove,
Were little cakes of sand.
My little friend from down the road,
Would come and visit me.
And we would sip from acorn cups,
Our fresh spring water tea.
She brought with her sweet flowers,
From the wild rose vine.
I'd share with her, things she liked,
From the treasures, that were mine.
With little brooms of cedar,
We swept my playhouse floor.
With pretty rocks, we lined the path,
That led up to the door.
When shadows from a setting sun,
Came streaking cross the sky.
I'd walk with her, half way home,
And there we'd say good-bye.

Next day I'd go and visit her,
We'd clean her play house too.
So happy was our childhood,
For we had so much to do.
We grew up and both were wed,
With time we grew apart.
But memories of my little friend,
Will live always in my heart.

CHIRSTMAS MEMORIES

———— ∞ ————

At Christmas Time my heart goes back to the Christmas times of yore.
When a homemade wreath of holly and fresh pine hung on our door.

The big log fire on Christmas Eve did never burn so bright.
And thoughts of seeing Santa Claus filled us with delight.

From the mantle piece new stockings hung. Papa said, "Sure as you're born,
fruit and nuts will be there, when you wake Christmas morn."

Our Christmas tree smelled beautiful. It made one feel so glad
to see the tinsel sparkle in the coal oil light we had.

Just in the hall hung mistletoe; no way to pass and miss.
You knew for sure if you came in, you were bound to get a kiss.

Our Christmas dinner was the best that Mama could prepare.
The welcome mat was always out for friends to come and share.

I know you all have memories down in your heart so dear.
So join this Christmas joys with those and fill the day with cheer.

BORN TOO LATE

———— ∞ ————

I wish I was the bride of a Cave man,
No sweeping to do, just sprinkle fresh sand.
No dishes to wash, when it is hot,
We'd eat with our fingers, out of one big pot.
No clothes to make, we'd sing a song,
And wait until a Bear came along.
There's food for all, with no bills to pay,
No saving up for that rainy day.
No books to learn, no bus to catch,
No windows to wash, no door to latch.
No one with nerves, no one taking pills,
No body bothered, with alcoholic chills.
When the weather is hot, no one would rave,
We'd move further back in the cool of the cave.
No delinquent kids, your heart to ache,
No cavities from eating, candy and cake.
In winter time, no froze up car,
We'd pass the time, getting wood for the fire.
No permanents to get, no hair to dye,
Your hair is for your mate, to lead you by.
No saving up to take a long trip,
To a foreign land, on a great big ship.
No life insurance, for the by and by,
To be collected, after you die.

Ethel Crownover

No rockets to build, no bombs to dread,
We could talk about the weather instead.
If we could turn back to beginning of man,
You'd see he had more than we ever can.
The world is getting worse for the Human Race,
Seems to me the beginning, 'twas a Heavenly Place.

SAVE OUR MOTHER EARTH

Our Mother Earth is crying,
She's hurting from the pain.
Of poison in our land and streams,
That fall in tears of rain.

Our Mother's heart is breaking,
Feel the quaking of the ground.
She's warning of what is to come,
From pollution all around.

Our bountiful waves of golden grain,
Will turn to dust and sand.
The trees will die, and streams go dry,
If we don't protect our land.

What goes up must come down,
You can't trust an incinerator.
To keep your air and water clean,
When greed is the regulator.

All living things depend on Earth,
There is no separation.
Our way of life well be destroyed,
With all our desecration.

Ethel Crownover

Dear God please save our Mother Earth,
Greatest of all your creations.
Don't let our Mother die,
From garbage incineration.

AWARDS OF HEAVEN

———— ∞ ————

In Heaven God's stage is all ready,
The audience sits waiting intense.
The chosen of God, have learned their parts well,
In their lives, there have been no pretense.

The awards soon will be given,
No envy will there by among them.
Already each knows the performance they gave,
And why they've been chosen by Him.

For Earth is a school of dramatics,
Where faith in your teacher pays off.
Your whole life is spent in the learning,
Each day filled with taunting and scoff.

To excel each day you must practice,
Lessons given by the Master above.
The greatest award, will be given to them,
That have majored in Brotherly Love.

GOOD OLD GOOSE FEATHERS

―――――――― ∞ ――――――――

Back home in the Winter time,
That upstairs room was cold.
I watched the snow, come sifting through a crack.
With Mama's old jeans quilt above,
And them good old warm goose feathers at my back.

With the moon I played peek-a-boo,
As the clouds went a scurrying.
I saw wild geese fly honking, cross the sky.
And I wondered what it's like up there,
And would I go there when I die.

I could hear the rats a scratching,
And a gnawing at the logs.
Trying to make a place to keep them warm.
And I prayed to my God above,
He wouldn't let them do me no harm.

I could hear the north wind whistling,
Round the corner of the house.
And the tree limbs as they'd freeze and pop and crack.
Then I was thankful for that old jeans quilt,
And them good old warm goose feathers at my back.

I could smell the ham a frying,
And the cedar wood a burning.
As my mama cooked our breakfast down below.
And when papa done the milking
I could hear his boots come crunching through the snow.

I just wish that life was tranquil,
As peaceful as then.
When I saw and heard my whole world through a crack.
With mama's quilt and God above,
And them good old warm goose feathers at my back.

I'M MARCHING

———— ∞ ————

I'm Marching, I'm Marching,
Down this long weary road.
The Black man he tell me,
That's how to ease my load.
The White man he tell me,
To stay put in my place.
The Black man he tell me,
March and lift up your race.
A poor man's a poor man,
His hungry children cry.
I'm a poor man, and will be,
Until the day I die.
Oh Lord! Oh dear Lord,
There's many such as I.
Does a poor man, does a black man,
Have a place up in your sky.
I'm Marching, I'm Marching,
Got nothing else to do.
This freedom I'm promised,
Can only come from you.
That White man he hates me,
I can see it in his face.
Reach down and help me,
Creator of my Race.

I'm Marching, I'm Marching,
I'm told that I'll be free.
The further I march,
The more misery I see.
This world's full of turmoil,
The clouds of unrest roll.
I march cause they're marching,
Dear Lord protect my Soul.

To Tommy

Little Imp with eyes of blue.
You're like me, and I'm like you.
Dancing, laughing, running wild.
I see myself again a child.

The world is bright, there's nothing wrong,
In rain or shine, your life's a song.
There's happiness in everything,
Never a frown, you always sing.

When I was young, my greatest joy,
Was wish and dream, I was a boy.
Believe my son and a wish comes true,
I see myself a boy in you.

JET SET SANTA

Santa Claus is coming soon,
To fill your hanging sock.
If Great-Grandpa could see him now,
He'd really get a shock.

For Santa isn't fat no more,
He's a singing, swinging Pal.
He has a color TV set,
And he's drinking Metracal.

He's slim and trim, and in the groove,
He's a real tough, jiving trick.
He doesn't have a beard no more,
His wife bought him a Schick.

He's turned the Reindeer out to roam,
That sleigh bit was all wet.
This year if you sit up and watch,
You'll see a zooming jet.

He doesn't come by chimney now,
All that was so in vain.
Instead of coke, leave by the door,
A quart of Pink Champagne.

For all the world has speeded up,
And Santa must keep the pace.
His job too, must modernize,
If he fills all the socks in space.

His tiny shop is now a plant,
He has an assembly line.
To be prepared for Christmas eve,
The Elves are working over time.

To make the toys, for girls and boys,
To fill up Santa's plane.
And get him on his yearly flight,
To bring cheer to the world again.

COUNTRY LIVING

―――――― ∞ ――――――

Walking down a country lane,
with the sun a setting cross the cotton field.
Been over to the neighbor's house,
Just to borrow us a mess of meal.

Wondering how hot tomorrow'll be,
Cause the sun a-setting in the West is red.
Got to hurry cause my mama
Is waiting for the meal to make the bread.

I can see the dust a-rising,
So I know my papa's still behind the plow.
I've got to do the feeding,
Then hunt and milk the roguish cow.

Old hound dog come from the hen house,
So meat and gravy's all we'll have to eat come morn'
But mama said we should be grateful
Just for the fact that we were born.

She says we should be thankful,
Cause lots of folks ain't got a bite to eat,
And we got 'taters in the cellar,
And in the smoke-house we still got lots of meat.

Dusk is slowly falling
Cool breezes slipping gently down the hill.
Night birds are a-calling,
I sure love to hear the Whip-o-will.

Cold milk is at the cave spring,
Got to get it while there is still light.
It sure will stop the hungries,
With that cornbread mama's cooking us tonight.

Cool sheets are awaiting,
First I'll thank the Lord,
For Keeping me from harm.
And if he plans,
For me another life,
I'll ask him please to let me,
Live it on the farm.

TODAY IT'S SPRING

———— ∞ ————

Today I saw a Bluebird ,
Sitting in a tree.
Today I saw a little bud,
As green as it could be.

Today I saw the Dandelions
Scattered everywhere.
Today my world was beautiful,
For Spring was in the air.

Today the sky was azure blue,
The breezes soft and sweet,
The fresh plowed ground kept calling,
For me to bear my feet.

The little creek was running full,
From the late March rain.
It gurgled as it sang to me,
"Springtime is here again."

Today I heard the little frogs,
Croaking loud and clear,
"Today our world is beautiful,
For Springtime is here."

Today I heard the Robin sing,
"Proclaim throughout the land,
Today the world is beautiful,
For God reached down his hand."

My Vision

———— ∞ ————

When I was a little girl, I guess my age was ten,
My daddy drove me way down South, to visit with a friend.

We ran to play behind the house, within a grove of trees,
And there the ruins of bygone days, stood fascinating me.

I felt the presence of the past, and then before my eyes,
A great mansion with pillars, and with lights came alive.

There in the garden stood a gentleman and a lady saying their good-byes,
I thought my heart would break for them as the tears shined in their eyes.

Within a Ball was going on, such splendor I'd never seen,
Outside Magnolias were in bloom; The lawn a satin green.

And then the vision went away; I stood forlorn and sad,
Until I saw in the lily pond, two frogs sitting on a pad.

Somehow I knew the same Great Power that had let me see the past,
Had intervened and let those two have their happiness at last.

THAT LITTLE ONE ROOM SCHOOLHOUSE

There are many times when I look back,
To that little one room school.
Where I learned to read and spell,
And write the Golden Rule.

When it was cold, I'd warm my hands,
On the little pail I'd take
With sausage, ham and biscuits hot,
And Mama's chocolate cake.

I walked a path most times alone.
And such wonders did I see.
The trees, the rocks and bright sunrise,
Just the birds, the squirrels and me.

We had no indoor plumbing,
No lunch room and no bus,
But our dedicated teacher,
Made us feel, she cared for us.

Our teacher was also the Janitor,
So we helped her all we could.
The boys carried in the coal.
And split the kindling wood.

The big girls helped the little ones,
Whose lessons were too hard.
We also swept the schoolhouse floor,
And cleaned the schoolhouse yard.

There wasn't many absentees,
No matter what the weather.
We were so few and all were friends,
And we wished to be together.

That little one room schoolhouse,
Is almost now extinct.
It was the greatest place to learn,
To read, spell, count and think.

THE WIDOWER'S PRAYER

Dear Lord, I am a widower,
I've abstained one year long.
But now, I'm lonesome, I want a wife
Could that wish be very wrong?

I don't want just anyone,
She must be, just right.
Just like my wife, take care of me,
And be there, with me at night.

She must not smoke those Cigarettes,
To use tobacco is a sin.
And another thing, I just Can't stand,
Is snuff dripping from her chin.

I'd like for her to be pretty and slim,
With black hair like my wife had.
She must wear lip stick and perfume,
And cheer me, when I'm sad.

I'd like her hips, sorta pleasantly plump,
And walk like a Percheron Mare.
Don't worry if she is getting grey,
I can always dye her hair.

And it would be nice if she drew a check.
So she could support herself.
By buying half of the groceries,
To replenish the pantry shelf.

Do you think, I'm a little too picky?
And my time is flying by?
Oh Lord, if I don't get a woman,
I know I'll surely die.

You say I'm too old for breeding,
That such thoughts are all in my head.
And one night, with what I've ordered
I'd roll off in the floor, stone cold dead.

I guess I have been too selfish,
I know I"m not smarter than you.
You know how man is, when desperate,
So any old hag will do.

THE HAIRCUT

———————— ∞ ————————

When I was just a little girl,
On the farm a-running wild.
I wondered why the neighbor lady,
Left me with her child.

She went a-peddling with my mama,
And with me, she left her there.
And to save her sight one day,
I said, "I'll cut your hair."

She had to bend her head way back
And peep beneath the bangs,
So that day I said to her,
"I'll shorten up them "thangs."

She sat real still while I cut,
Till I ran out of hair.
She looked just like a Pussy Cat,
That had fought a bear!

When I saw what I had done,
I said, "What can I do?"
I'll drill you till, you learn to say,
Taylor did this thing to you.

I'd yell out, "Who cut your hair?"
"Taylor," said she in her sweet voice.
After all, he was my 'favorite' brother,
And besides, I had no choice.

When her mother screamed,
"Who cut you hair?"
"Taylor," the sweet child said.
But when HE asked, "Who said I did?'
I knew that I was dead!!!

INFLATION IN STORYBOOK LAND

———— ∞ ————

Let me tell you about storybook land,
Since inflation is out of hand.
Milk is now the highest,
Since old Bossy jumped the moon.
The dish has minted into coin,
The silver in the spoon.
The wolf is standing at the door.
But he will not come in.
He's afraid the little pigs,
Will make a roast of him.
Miss Muffet on her tuffet sat,
To eat her curds and whey,
The spider said, I must be off,
She's had no meat today.
Jack Horner in his corner sat,
He said I think I'll cry.
I have no place to stick my thumb,
Some one has ate my pie.
King Cole is not a merry old soul,
For now he has to shout.
Phone rates soared, he couldn't pay,
So his phone was taken out.
Poor Mother Goose is all alone,
No more does she wander.

Feathers is all she has left,
Some one ate her Gander.
The King has nothing left to count,
The Queen spent all his money.
She made a trip into town,
And bought a quart of honey.
Poor Bo Peep has lost her sheep,
But there's no need her looking.
Jack Sprat and his wife,
Have got them on a cooking.
Mary, Mary still contrary,
But flowers she doesn't grow.
To bring her food budget down,
Planted potatoes in the row.
Jack is nimble, Jack is quick,
But Jack is in a pout.
Congress introduced a bill,
To blow his candle out.
The moral of this poem is,
If one wants enough to eat,
Each be like the little Red Hen,
And plant a grain of wheat.

GOOD-BYE MY LOVE

I know I told you just to call,
If you found some one new.
But that was long before I learned,
How much that I loved you.

From the first I knew one day,
I would get this call.
I never realized how far,
A broken heart could fall.

I knew that your love for me,
Was not as strong as mine.
I only hoped with passing days,
It would increase with time.

Love is such a fragile thing,
With bands of steel that bind.
A feeling that comes from the heart,
It comes not from the mind.

It's not that you love me less,
Just that you love her more.
You say she's some one from your past,
That you once loved before.

My love is unselfish,
Although I love you so.
I see the writing on the wall,
It's time that I let go.

I only want your happiness,
If it cannot be with me,
If it lies with some one else,
What is to be will be.

Love cannot be measured,
And it is in control.
It is the master of your heart,
Embedded in your soul.

You know that I'll miss you,
In my arms at night in bed.
And I'll know that some where else,
You'll be in hers instead.

If this new love starts to fade,
Not what you want at all.
My love will still be waiting,
Waiting for your call.

Now if you wish we'll say good-bye,
And I'll face the lonely years.
With loving memories kept alive,
Refreshed with falling tears.

LIFE IS LIKE A CRUISE SHIP

Life is like a cruise ship,
And we're all there together.
Sailing on the sea of life,
In all kinds of weather.

If you are down in steerage,
Where life is not sublime,
If you make it, to top deck,
You'll have to learn to climb.

There is a ladder, that goes up.
Be careful you don't slip.
Just use the talent, that you have,
And become, Captain of your ship.

For the world is out there before you,
And is whirling round and round.
Your cruise ship, can circle it,
And never go aground.

A new life starts each sunrise,
There's nothing you can't be.
If you guide your ship, just right,
You'll sail a silver sea.

For life is like a cruise ship,
Where you go, you're free to choose,
You're at the helm, it's up to you,
If you wish, to win or lose.

HELLO LORD, I'M BILL CLINTON

———— ∞ ————

Hello Lord, I'm Bill Clinton,
I'm here to come within.
But first you say I must stand here,
And confess to you my sin.

Well you already know I smoked pot,
When I was very young.
And you know I was elected President,
With Hillary's help and my slick tongue.

I don't think my chasing skirts,
Should make you look at me with vex.
The fault is your greatest gift to man,
It was you invented sex.

I could easily forget dodging the draft,
If about it so many quit crying.
The draft was much safer to dodge,
Than all them bullets a flying.

Lets blame Whitewater on Hillary,
For she's quite a bossy girl.
And I have such a generous heart,
I've sent money all over the world.

And that Bosnia thing, I didn't know,
Would backfire in my face.
I thought they were joking about those mines,
Blowing troops all over the place.

Every ones entitled to one mistake,
And I think I'm becoming a bore.
So please forgive my biggest mistake,
And that was listening to Gore.

Well Bill, I'll have to let you in,
Though you sure haven't done too well,
The Devil called and said, don't send him here,
With his record he'll screw up Hell.

CHRISTMAS LONG AGO

I'd like to have another Christmas,
As we did long, long ago.
When Santa came and filled our socks,
With the best things in the toe.

At Christmas time we made a wreath,
Of holly for the door.
With Paraffin and kerosene,
We waxed the kitchen floor.

A week ahead my Mama baked,
And stored cakes in a can.
If you were good and carried wood,
You got to lick the pan.

We never had a Turkey,
But Mama baked a hen.
She never asked white meat or dark,
She dipped till you said when.

Happiness was every where,
In all the country round.
The only thing we wished for,
Was a big snow on the ground.

With silver painted sweet gum balls,
Our Christmas tree did shine.
Ropes made of fresh popped corn,
The cedar limbs entwined.

Colored paper in a chain,
Brightened up the tree,
A paper Angel at the top,
Would smile down at me.

For Christmas was a happy time,
But now it would be shocking,
If the only gift one should get.
Could be stuffed in a stocking.

MY MAGICAL ROOM

———— ∞ ————

Once I imagined a magical room
A beautiful magical room,
I could sit in the sun, look out on the world,
And talk to the man in the moon.

My beautiful, magical room was up high,
Such magic I felt, when up there.
Through the window, the breezes came dancing in,
And toyed with the strands of my hair.

Outside my window, raindrops pitter, patter,
Laughing and sliding with glee.
I looked out, at their funny little faces,
And they looked in at me.

Through my beautiful window I could see far,
And view wondrous things, just for me.
The Great Wall of China, at my finger tips,
And ships on a grassy green sea.

If you are unhappy, and your life is boring,
And filled with depression and gloom,
Just lay all your worries and troubles aside,
And imagine a magical room.

FOR HE WHO IS BALDING

Back in them Depression Days
We was poor as we could be.
We didn't even have a milking stool,
So Ma milked down on one knee.

Don't know how long it took,
Till Ma said, "There's something wrong,
Growing on my milking knee
Is black hair, two inches long."

Each time she milked, she scrubbed,
That knee with its head of hair.
The lye soap made it silky black.
We had never heard of Nair.

I said, "Ma it's the pressure,
In the barnyard dirt makes it grow."
Pa made a stool from the out house door,
He said, "That hairy knee's got to go."

Now my advice to balding men,
To grow hair I'll till you how.
Twice a day at the barn, stand on your head,
Long enough to milk a cow.

PRICE OF PROGRESS

———— ∞ ————

They built a Super Highway,
Cross the path I used to run.
Down to the one room school house,
Where we had so much fun.

They said that it was progress,
And that's what life's all about.
But that Super highway, Chopped a part,
Of my childhood out.

A bubbly spring ran by the path,
Into a crystal pool.
I sat and talked there, with the frogs,
About my day at school.

I told them all my problems,
And we solved everyone.
And they never, ever criticized
A single thing I'd done.

A rock there was my golden throne,
With a mossy carpet green.
They were my loyal subjects,
And I their Fairy Queen.

They shared with me, my fantasy,
And I their life with them.
They listened to the things, I'd say,
I watched them dive and swim.

They helped me through the troubled times,
We all have getting grown.
When with friends, I'd need to talk,
None better have I known.

I told them that a wicked witch,
Had made them that way.
And I promised them, that I,
Would break her spell one day.

They taught me that contentment.
Was a state of mind,
And that happiness, was there,
Within ones self to find.

I wish they had understood,
The things that I would say.
And so perhaps, I could explain,
Why our world was swept away.

A PRAYER OF THANKS

———— ∽ ————

Dear Lord if I choose to pray,
At early morn or close of day.
What is it I should ask of you,
When up above, the sky is blue.
All I possess, I do not own,
You gave it to me, as a loan.

How can I be displeased or sad,
When everything is bright and glad.
To feel the wind, and see the sun,
And moon and stars, when day is done.
What man has made, is not for me,
The things I want, the most are free.

If forever and a day I live,
I can't see all, the things you give.
To everyone, to use each day,
To love, enjoy in their own way.
So when I get, on bended knee,
It's to give thanks, for being free.

MY FATHER I THANK YOU

My Father in Heaven, I pray to thank you,
For the sky up above, that is shining so blue.
For the little raindrops, that so gently fall,
And the fluffy white kitten, that comes when I call.
For the beautiful flowers, the birds and the trees,
The air that is sweetened, by a fresh mountain breeze.
For the little children, that laugh as they play,
And the glorious night, that follows the day.

My Father in Heaven, I kneel when I pray,
To give thanks for the dawn, of another day.
For the grass so green, sparkling with dew,
In this most wonderful world created by you.
My Father I thank Thee, for the Son that you gave,
To all of mankind, and for my soul to save.
Each day and each hour, I give thanks to Thee,
And for the ultimate sacrifice, Christ made for me.

MY DREAM

———— ∞ ————

I was sitting in the moonlight,
And I must have fell asleep.
When a silver moon beam,
Across my face did sweep.

Shaped like a great staircase.
I was trembling, in my knees,
I thought, I'll climb up and see,
If the moon, is made of cheese.

I don't know, how long I climbed.
To the moon, so big and bright.
By the time, I'd reached the top.
I'd lost all my fright.

Within a crater, on the moon,
Such a sight, I'd never seen,
Dancing on a silver floor,
Were little folks, of green.

They didn't mind my watching.
And one of them, climbed up,
To give me a drink of honey dew,
In a little silver cup.

I asked, what is your secret.
Of such happiness, in you land.
All together, they answered me.
Love your fellow man.

They sang and danced, around me,
Until the break of dawn.
With the first rays of the sun,
The little folks were gone.

That really, was a Super Dream,
I thought as, I waked up.
But there beside me on the grass,
Was a little silver cup.

TODAY MY HUSBAND PASSED AWAY

———————— ∞ ————————

Today my husband passed away.
He's gone to his reward.
I know exactly what he'll say,
When he goes to meet the Lord.

He'll yell St. Peter ! Open Up!!
Come on and let me in.
You say I must talk to the Lord,
About my worldly sin?

Dear Lord you know, I had to drink,
To prove I was a man.
And then when I got started,
It just got out of hand.

You say you know, I beat my wife.
Dear Lord that gives me chills.
But that was cause, she wanted me,
To help her pay the bills.

And now, you tell me gambling's wrong.
You say that too is sin.
This place is like the one I left.
There's no way I can win.

And about all them girls I chased.
That was a merry life.
You say you think, that was wrong,
Just because I had a wife.

And about all them other things.
We won't discuss them now,
Nor later either, cause it won't
Help my case any how.

Dear Lord, I'm getting mighty hot.
Please let me come inside.
You say, I must go down below,
For that's where I'll abide.

Today my husband passed away.
I sure do wish him well.
By dying he has set me free,
And took my place in Hell.

MAMA WHY DO YOU CRY?

Oh Mama please tell me,
About the mountains.
When they were pretty and green.
And of the creatures, that romped in the wood lands,
And things, that I've never seen.

Before incinerators, when you played, in the river.
And watched, the fish swimming by.
Oh Mama, please tell me, whatever happened.
To make such wondrous things die.

And tell me of the beautiful butterflies.
That flit and fly like a bird on the wing.
And the pure white snow you had in winter,
And the glorious coming of Spring.

Tell me about how you played, in the raindrops,
Why is it, I can't do that too.
And why don't you smile, when you tell,
Of the wonderful things, you used to do.

Of if I could have lived, in that magical time.
When birds sang and air, was so sweet.
You must have been happy in the spring time.

When you ran through plowed ground with bare feet.

Mama please tell me, with such beautiful memories,
When you talk, why do you cry?
Is is because, like the birds and mountains,
You think God, will soon let me die.

MAJESTIC MOUTAIN

———— ⚭ ————

Majestic as your peaks reach out,
To mingle with the clouds on high.
From way up there I love to look,
To where your spreading foothills lie.

On Summer days in ferny glade.
So soul inspiring just to be.
Alone for hours, beneath your shade,
From wordly ties I'm free.

You're clothed in beauty always new.
Each day a change in everyplace.
Murmuring streams, flowing by,
Add to the charm of your grace.

Beneath the shelter of your trees,
God's creatures all have room to roam,
And gather food that you provide.
'Neath rocks and brush, they build a home.

You were created, just as we,
But you will never die.
With changing seasons, you'll always be,
More beautiful as time goes by.

The tender green of early spring,
We think you can't compare.
The flowers bloom, the earth grows warm,
And summer slips in unaware.

Before our eyes, you change your clothes,
And then before we know,
In colors no tongue can describe.
You're decked out in an Autumn glow.

You drop your leaves as days grow short.
For time has come for all to rest.
Your changing beauty now has grown,
As pure white snow, falls on your breast.

And there you'll stand majestically,
In beauty as the years roll by.
For all to see, who wish, enjoy,
And share your wonders just as I.

DIVORCE! REALLY!

———————— ∞ ————————

Dear Wife, I think we should divorce,
I'm tired of being wed.
Once more I wish to be footloose,
And be free instead.

Dear husband, you disturb me much,
And you almost make me mad.
What do you, propose to do,
With these four kids we've had?

You say you'll pay me child support.
Please will you tell me how,
You'll do something, when you're gone,
That you're not doing now.

You say you wish me to be true.
While you have a brand new bride.
So if you wish, you can come back
If you're not satisfied.

Dear husband, we will be divorced.
If you wish that it will be.
But I'll be the one, that is footloose,
I'll be the one that is free.

For I have been a faithful wife,
These children belong to you.
I'll give you custody of the kids,
And pay alimony too.

And about my being true to you,
Till you know, your choice is right.
I promise there'll be another head,
On your pillow by tonight.

You say you have changed your mind,
Before you've even gone.
The game's the same, but rules have changed.
I'll rule this roost, from now on.

OLD LADY AND HER CAT

———————— ∞ ————————

Together on the couch, they nap,
She all stretched out, he on her lap.
For many months, since just a kitten,
With one another, they've been smitten.
The love they have, is plain to see,
He on her lap, head on her knee.
She strokes his back, and he will Purr,
And with a paw, he will stroke her.
It matters not, that she's grown old,
For cats have, nine lives, I'm told.
The greatest thing in life, they've found,
That love makes, the world go' round.
Between the two, there is no gap.
She all stretched out, he on her lap.

LITTLE BOY ON LABOR DAY

With books and lunch beside the road,
He stands and waits and wonders why,
The bus he rides, just doesn't come.
It's Labor Day, Poor little guy.

I passed at nine and thought,
I'll bet he didn't hear.
When teacher said, that Labor Day,
Would be a holiday this year.

I wonder now, how many things,
In life have passed me by.
Because my ears, had gone to sleep
With birds my mind soared in the sky.

And even now I cannot say,
Which is the best to do.
To hear and see and know it all,
or jus the things that interest you.

I know that I have laughed and dreamed,
Of the wonders of Heaven and Earth.
But lonely days, not one I've lived.
They've all been filled with mirth.

Ethel Crownover

As years pass by and you grow old,
No one will know but you.
If you have lived your life in full,
Or passed by things, you wished to do.

LITTLE SENIOR GIRL

———— ∞ ————

Happy little Senior girl.
Ready to give this life a whirl.
Leaving behind your greatest joy,
That happy-go-lucky Senior boy.

Out into the stream of life,
To college, to prepare for strife,
That faces you as on you go,
To learn things, you now don't know.

Be careful in the life you choose.
A precious lot, you've got to lose.
Your future new, that looks so bright,
With one misstep, be black as night.

Choose not the way that you will take,
Because it looks well trod.
The narrow, unworn path is safe,
If you are led by God.

THE SOUTH'S GONNA RISE AGAIN

I've always heard it said,
From time I don't know when,
Save your Confederate money boys,
Cause the South's gonna rise again.

When Sherman marched through Georgia,
All the way down to the sea.
He didn't have no crystal ball.
To see what was to be.

He couldn't see a southern gentle man,
With his lady by his side,
Elected by the nation.
In the white house to reside.

It took a hundred years to get there,
Some folks are quite upsot,
That the South's done took the White House,
And we didn't even fire a shot.

Now when you tour the White House,
You'll hear a Southern drawl,
Say come right in, and set a spell,
And howdy to you all.

If you smell a sweet aroma,
Like a breeze from off the sea,
If you hail from down in Dixie
You'll know it's Sassafras Tea.

We've always heard of Protocol,
But don't know what it be.
It can't do half as much
As Southern hospitality.

You don't borrow from a neighbor,
If you got as much as he.
That Southern rule, we got to teach,
To our friends across the sea.

We are sailing troubled waters,
With a new Captain at the prow.
That knows how to live on peanuts,
And he's gonna teach us how.

LOVE NOT LIBERATE

———— ∞ ————

This liberation movement
Don't sound to me like fun.
I think it was started by,
An old maid and a nun.

They think you'll turn loose your guy,
And they'll catch him if they can.
You may fool some, but not me gals,
I'm sticking with my man.

I'd hate to think, I'd be treated,
Like some men I know.
They stay home and fight the kids,
While the wife goes to a show.

There's women got, just one old dress,
And some live in a shack.
But you couldn't swap a penthouse,
For what's sleeping at their back.

Don't be impressed, by their manly dress,
And their liberation cries.
They've no sex appeal, and they're out to steal,
See that man hungry look in their eyes.

So wise up girls, statistics show,
Too many women for every man.
Them liberation dolls, are on the prowl,
And they'll get yours if they can.

There's just no way to equalize,
The two can't be the same.
And if you'll just stop and think,
You won't want to change the game.

RAINY DAY REMINISCINHG

———— ∞ ————

Oh just to be, in a barn of hay,
On a rainy, rainy day.
To lie and rest beneath the tin,
Of the old barn roof, and hear the din,
Of the patter, patter of the big rain drops,
That lull you to sleep, before it stops.

The time has gone, and passed away,
When with a fork ,we pitched the hay.
It was soft and sweet and cured by the sun,
With time and care the haying was done.
Now it's baled in a rush, its hard and cold,
Just another product for getting gold.

Our land has become, a ball of speed,
Every way you turn, there is only greed.
Will we never have time, once more to stop,
In the hay, and listen to the big rain drops.

To Katherine

―――――― ∽ ――――――

With laughter like a Silver Bell,
That tinkled everywhere.
And a smile for everyone,
As she flitted here and there.

Her thoughts were always for her friends,
She lived just for today,
Her happiness, I'll ne'er forget.
She was so bright and gay.

The Christmas season was the time,
She loved the best of all.
The songs of sleighs and holidays,
Her memory does recall.

The shiny tinsel on the tree.
And bright lights hanging round,
Will always bring to all of us,
Dear memories of Katherine Brown.

IF YOU'VE NEVER MADE MOLASSES

―――――― ∽ ――――――

If you've never licked the skimmings, from a joint of Sorghum Cane.
You've got a lot left in life to do.
If you've never run up and slid down, a pile of Sorghum Pumas.
That's another thrill awaiting you.

Papa waked us early, the day he cooked the Sorghum,
He said kids you got to help me all you can.
With the stripping and the cutting,
The hauling and the grinding.

It takes work to get them cooking in the pan.
He knowed we never minded,
Cause we seldom ever, got a chance to miss a day of school.
Education was important, but the farm work, had to come first as a rule.

If you've never smelled molasses, on a clear, cold, frosty morning.
When they're being run off in a can.
There's no way I can tell you, words cannot describe it,
It's the sweetest smell in all the land.

If you've never kissed your sweetheart, at a lasses pull.,
You don't know how sweet, a kiss can be.
That's how I got my first love, with sticky lips and fingers,
And he's never got away from me.

If you've never had new lasses, stirred in fresh churned butter,.
And eat them on a biscuit while its hot.
You may have fame and fortune,
But in life, you have still missed quite a lot.

MY UNCLE'S WIFE

———— ∽ ————

Let me tell you about this woman.
My Daddy's youngest brother, chanced to wed.
He didn't have no education,
But she was a college grad they said.

She was big and strong and healthy,
And stout enough, to all day pull a plow.
But when it come to cooking, and when it come to washing,
Them was two things, she just did not know how.

Sometimes her education,
With the farm work got in the way,
Like the time she cooked laying mash,
For the boys that were there haulng hay.

When I saw my Grandpa,
I thought with him, I'd have a friendly jest.
I said what were you doing,
Trying to get on that old Red hen's nest.

He said if you think that's funny,
There's another thing, I'd like for you to know.
Each time I pass the hen house,
I have this urge, to flap my arms and crow.

Sex was her favorite subject,
And forever had it classed as sin.
Uncle waited patiently,
And hoped some day, she'd tell him when.

Uncle said things will get better,
There's just no way it can get worse.
He was right, for just last week.
They come and got him in a hearse.

ALL THIS BY GREYHOUND BUS

If life with your mate gets boring,
And you're inclined to fuss.
Just get yourself a ticket,
And take a trip by Greyhound bus.

I took a vacation trip,
Out to the great Northwest.
To see a little scenery,
And to get a little rest.

I met this gal in Spokane,
I thought with her I'll chat.
Before one word, I could speak,
She started, just like that.

"I have a Mama six feet tall,
She weights four hundred pounds.
My Dad is only five foot four,
And just twelve inches round.

I've had my kids all summer long,
They've almost drove me mad.
From Seattle, I'm on my way to Butte,
To visit Mom and Dad.

My husband left me with two kids,
I could find no trace of him.
Again I married and pretty soon,
He adopted them.

We had three and that made five,
I couldn't stand the strain.
We were divorced, I gave him all,
And I was free again.

One day I said my life a drag,
I think I'll marry up.
So now I have a husband blind,
And a half grown Great Dane pup.

My second husband married too,
I said that's really fine.
The wife he chose, had four kids,
So he wound up with nine.

I keep my kids three months a year.
I help to buy their clothes.
Their step-mother waved good-bye today,
With her thumb against her nose.

My pride and joy is happy now,
With no kids on the place.
He runs and jumps up in the bed,
And licks us in the face."

Just like the man with the Albatross,
Hanging round his neck.

She told of the fights with the kids and the dog,
And all this with sound effects.

All night long she rambled on,
About the kids and the Great Dane pup.
The driver said, "I've had enough,
Why the Hell, don't she shut up."

In Butte, we went our separate ways
As I got on my bus to ride.
In sympathy, I turned and waved good-bye,
To the new Victim by her side.

SERENITY MOUNTAIN

———— ∞ ————

Up on the mountain, wild and high,
I stop to hear the Rain Crow cry.
The music of a thousand things,
Makes me rejoice, the whole world sings.

I hear the buzzing of a bee,
Two squirrels a chattering in a tree.
I stir and every thing goes still,
And from the quiet I get a thrill.

So glad am I to hear and see,
The splendor God has given me.
In sunset glow from yonder hill,
I hear the song of Whip-O-Will.

How wonderful his joy to share,
He sings on without a care.
Simple life was meant to be,
God's creatures all but man can see.

He alone from all the rest,
With discontentment in his breast.
Promotes more hatred year, by year,
And all the world must live in fear.

To Evyonne

————— ∞ —————

I know you will think this is silly,
And will say, she just thinks she can write verse.
But one day you'll look back, and read it again,
And will say somewhere, I've read worse.

Your life lies out there before you,
And till now it's been free all the way.
But it's a tough pull to the top of the hill,
When you must battle it out everyday.

To be great you have to be different,
Don't identify yourself with the crowd.
You can't see the wheat, if mixed in the chaff,
So stand out alone and be proud.

Don't leave a footprint, on the back of a friend,
And make one for each of life's miles.
For it is so easy, to say some kind words,
And flash a few friendly smiles.

Everyone is searching for something,
If its happiness, it is there with in.
So cheer up the world with your lovely face,
Start a happiness epidemic, give a grin.

There is nothing so rewarding as kindness,
And no matter how lowly the plight.
The rich and the poor, alike are both drawn,
To a face, with a smile all a light.

A FISHER WIFE'S WISH

———— ∞ ————

Good Fairy grant to me one wish,
One glorious day without a fish.
Hooked to a string,
Brought through the door,
With fishy drippings on the floor.

My husband, son, and every friend,
Just fish and fish there seems no end.
Then through the door,
They charge with glee,
And hold them high for all to see.

Time races on, in dark or light,
There's always one more fish to bite.
Not one they catch, looks like the other,
Come look! good wife,
Get up dear Mother.

From deepest slumber, I come awake,
To noise of thunder, and clashing quake.
I just turn over,
I have no fear,

I know my fishing men are here.
From early morn until its late,
They talk of reels and lines and bait.
Good Fairy, let me get one drink, without fish thrashing in the sink.
And one whole day, my lungs to swell,
With air, without a fishy smell.

THE RETURN

Long years ago, I went away.
It seems to me like yesterday.
Just sixty years between have flown.
Yet all my friends, round here are gone.

I found the grave of my dear Mother.
My. Sister, Father and my Brother.
The places where I ran at play.
All rotten, weedy, washed away.
The village that was quite a town.
Is nothing, everything torn down.
Only the bend the river had.
Was there to make, my tired heart glad.

Four friends left, from all I knew.
And like the town, they'd faded too.
Oh how I wish, I'd stayed away.
And remembered this, as yesterday.

WHEN TWO FORDS MET

―――――― ∞ ――――――

While driving home from work last night,
With my little Brothers two.
We took the short way by the Fiord,
The natural thing to do.

I saw the creek was kinda wide.
And the water swift and brown.
But never once, did I think,
It was deep enough to drown.

The truck went splashing, sinking fast.
I held the wheel so brave.
Until the water came so high.
I reached out to pat a wave.

Higher still the water came.
Inside the cab it poured.
"Sit still and drown," Tommy cried.
But I'm jumping overboard,

I saved him from a watery grave.
I pulled him in the bed.
And with my other hand I held.
My picture frame above my head.

Books and papers floated by.
The boys did swim them down.
All our possessions we must save.
Even if we had to drown.

Safe and dry at home we are.
The old Ford truck's still wet.
As time goes by, the truck will dry.
And forever I'll remember when two Fords met.

LAURA'S ANSWERING SERVICE

Today I went to see a friend,
I think most of you know her.
Her car was sitting parked outside,
So I knocked upon her door.

I waited and I peeked within,
I saw no one in sight.
I said I think I'll, clang her bell,
For she has slept the night.

I gave a clang, to my surprise,
Out dropped a spider grim.
I didn't scream, but he could tell,
That I was scared of him.

I peeked inside, I saw no one,
I gave another ring.
Out dropped my spider friend again,
Upon another string.

With fingers sticking in his ears,
I could plainly see.
His second answer to my ring,
Was one too much for me.

Ethel Crownover

I said good-bye, and tell my friend,
When she gets back home.
Her answering service is too far out,
I'll call her on the phone.

JOURNEY TO MEMPHIS STATE

We started out to Memphis State,
One morning bright and gay.
But Lizzie slowed our progress down,
She gagged all the way.

At last our journey's end was reached,
No motels were in sight.
The phone booth was too soured to use,
To save us from our plight.

We drove along through traffic thick,
And there came in our view.
Most welcome sight to weary eyes,
Good luck to us, "Oh Silver Horseshoe".

Our thoughts ran first to washing up,
To rest from traveler's strain.
But Cathy did so recklessly,
Comb her gold earring down the drain.

For help I went, unthoughtedly,
I placed my life in danger.
Three hundred miles away from home,
And I was riding with a stranger.

It's truly sure the Lord above,
Looks after fools, that cannot see.
I wondered where, I would be found.
When he finished killing me.

But no, he was a gentleman,
I've heard they're most extinct.
He got his tools, brought me back,
And rescued the earring from the sink.

Oh Memphis State you'll educate.
Long after we are dead.
Lizzie and I will never attend,
We'll just be ignorant instead.

MOTEL CONFUSION

———— ∞ ————

Last night of vacation,
Our bus was running late.
At a local McDonalds,
Our supper we ate.

The Holiday Inn,
Like an old railroad station.
Was the most confusing,
In all the nation.

If your room was two,
You went back down to one.
If you were up on six,
You found you had none.

If you were on four,
You went back down to two.
And met all the folks,
That didn't know what to do.

Our tour guide was running,
Up and down the hall.
Saying, "How the heck in the morning,
Will I find you all?"

Ethel Crownover

At breakfast rain was dripping,
So you ran through the wet.
For the dining car hadn't,
Got to the depot yet.

Of all your vacations,
I'm sure you will say.
Motel confusion, the most confusing,
Place, you ever did stay.

RECYCLING

———— ∞ ————

Them Depression Days, sure was bad.
So we recycled everything we had.
We saved the cob, when we shelled the corn.
It came in handy on a frosty morn.
The Sears Catalog it would replace.
When out back you had to race.
Its use wasn't over, we saved that too.
To make a hot fire, under the stew.
It made the kitchen so toasty warm.
When with a chill, you came from the barn.
We praised that cob, when put to the test.
It's many uses, sure were the best.
Then Mama said, "Sure as you're born,
Them ashes will slip the skin off the corn."
So them ashes wound up in the hominy vat.
When it comes to recycling, try and beat that.
But Mama said, "Wait, we ain't done.
The garden gets what's left.
At rising of the sun."

BE HAPPY

———— ∞ ————

One day St. Peter, said to God,
Dear God, what shall I do?
When the Golden Gate is opened up,
Disgruntled folks, come rushing through.

They start to tell, what's been took out,
By doctor's here and there.
And then, they look around and ask,
Where is my rocking chair?

I try to tell them that up here,
Bodies have no need for rest.
They look at me disappointedly,
And say, You surely jest.

If I can't tell the folks I meet,
How my gallstones were taken out.
My stomach stapled and my face lifted,
What will we talk about?

I tell them this is Heaven,
Where birds sing, and flowers grow.
If a nursing home is what you want,
You must go back down below.

What we want here, is a smiling face,
From one, though their life was hard.
Was ready to face, each day head on,
And never said, I'm just too tired.
No one wants to hear your ailments,
Or how your operation was done.
Somewhere, sometime, you've walked in the woods,
And with a friend watched a setting sun.

THE EASTER BUNNY

———————— ∞ ————————

Mama asked the little bunny,
Why on Easter morn you're gone.
And I have to hide my eggs,
And then hunt them all alone.

I wish you would hide them for me,
Wake me, when you are done.
While you watch, I'll hop and hunt them,
I think that would be such fun.

Darling always, Easter morning,
The easter Bunny's honor bound.
To color pretty eggs for children,
And hide them, everywhere around.

Someday soon, you will replace me,
That is why, You must learn now.
To color pretty eggs and hide them.
So in the future, you'll know how.

Just think what a sorry, sad place,
If a little boy or girl.
Didn't have an Easter Bunny,
To help brighten up their world.

FOOD STAMP BOOGER

———— ∞ ————

I happened in behind a gal,
In a grocery store today.
And while the clerk ran up her bill,
She laid out her stamps to pay.

The cart was filled up to the top,
And there to my surprise.
Very neatly packaged,
Lay a whole hog before my eyes.

Such chops and roasts, I'd never seen,
No part did she leave out.
She could have put it together again,
She had the feet through to the snout.

And that wasn't all she had,
There lay a half a bull.
She would have got the other half,
But her shopping cart was full.

I looked in vain for a bag of beans,
Or just one tiny tater.
As she replaced her stack of stamps,
In her bag of alligator.

There must be something mighty wrong,
When the poor are so better fed.
Than we, who work and pay the tax,
While they, relax in bed.

Marie Antoinette lost her head,
For suggesting the poor eat cake.
But seems to me, it's the other extreme,
For us to feed them steak.

They seldom ever pass the draft,
Is it because they lay and snooze.
Or do you think, they swap the meat,
For a quart or two of booze.

Why don't we just divide them up,
Since we've got them on our backs.
And count them as dependents,
When we figure our income tax.

They keep increasing more and more,
And we, keep dwindling away.
What's to become of our great land,
When there's no one left to pay.

Our Country now is floundering,
Just like a broken ship.
The middle class can't keep it up,
With only them to dip.

The working class is taxed to death.,
They're done pushed to the brink.
Unless the rich and poor help out,
Our whole great land will sink.

THIS IS MY LIFE

———— ∾ ————

This is my life God gave to me.
To do that which, I wish to do.
It is mine and mine alone.
Like yours, belongs to you.

I took a vow, I said I'd share.
I didn't say, I'd give.
The greatest gift God gave to me.
My right, my life to live.

Into my world, I go alone.
Where I have time to think.
In life's fountain, I can wade.
Its cool waters, I can drink.

I can't be ruled, nor possessed.
That's not how life should be.
For deep within the soul of all,
Is that longing to be free.

This is my life, this is my world.
On the beach in the sands of time.
When I look back at the foot prints,
I see yours, but I must also see mine.

AWAKEN! TAXPAYERS!

———— ∞ ————

Franklin County's on the move,
To build, to grow, to climb.
But in their walls, a big termite,
Sits waiting, to steal them blind.
With grimy claws in county funds,
He smokes a big cigar.
With county funds, he buys the gas.
To drive a big, black car.
For many years, we all had hoped,
That he would surely die.
I do believe, if he were dead,
He still could steal and lie.
Each day he goes and eats two meals,
From food for which we pay.
He thinks the hospital is his egg,
And he sits there day by day.
When will this land stand up and shake,
This termite from it's breast.
He has us at the bankrupt point,
Shall we let him have the rest?
He got the funds, we raised to build,
A hospital for the poor.
This Tims Ford Dam is a sure thing.
He's reaching out for more.

Ethel Crownover

Our county government is corrupt.
Don't tell yourself, it's not.
Wake up and stand, and be a man.
Cut out the weeds and rot.
Do you attend our County Court,
To see the farce that's made?
Our J.P.'s sleep while graft goes on,
And padded bills are paid.
I'm only one, but I can see,
If our county stays together.
The time is now to straighten out.
Or be divided up forever.

DEAR DAD

———— ∞ ————

Dear Dad, my heart is a window.
Looking back into a world.
Where together we all were so happy.
And I was my Daddy's girl.

Your face with a smile I remember.
It has become so important to me.
Shining so bright, until I was grown.
From the time I clung to your knee.

Dear Dad, there's no way to tell you.
The sorrow your absence has brought.
Our love has not lessened, because you're away.
Nor have we forgotten a thing that you taught.

I pray that someday all together,
That God, will grant it to be.
We'll meet you Dad, just as you were.
With a smile on your face, just for me.

TRUST YOUR MULE

A man of the mountains,
Is nobodies fool.
Instead of a horse,
He rides a mule.

He knows his mule,
Is on the ball.
He never stumbles,
And he never falls.

That mountain is high,
And steep is the bluff.
But that little muley,
Sure knows his stuff.

Steady is his footsteps.
And cool is his head.
Where just one miss step,
You'd both wind up dead.

Back in these mountains,
Men have one golden rule.
Though you don't trust you woman,
You can sure trust your mule.

A HOUSE WITH NO CURTAINS

———— ∞ ————

I grew up in a house with no curtains.
Through the window the whole world to see.
The wealth inside, was love for each other.
And the happiest inmate, 'neath that roof, was me.

Freedom was not just a word in a manual.
We were taught what, it was meant to be.
Your God given right to pursuit of happiness,
I learned as I clung to my Daddy's knee.

Through that window today, I see no smiling faces.
The freedom that once was, is dwindling away.
Folks are pursuing, things that don't matter.
All the glitter is gone, at close of the day.

Farther away may God let me wander.
Back to a house, where windows are bare.
Back to a time when people were happy,
To a freedom once more, when we had time to share.

Someway, somehow, we must pull back the curtains.
For those that want to can look out and see.
If freedom is lost, it will be gone forever,
From the people once known, as the brave and the free.

NO MORE VACATION

It seems vacations are not for me.
My dog was terrible mad at me.
Upset and nervous as he could be.
Had even pissed on every tree.

The goats said we thought you were dead.
So we ate one wall from off the shed.
You must never go away again.
Because you were gone it didn't rain.

When you are gone all is not well.
The sun beamed down hotter than Hell.
The weeds are wilted, the grass is dead.
We are thinking of finishing up the shed.

You know those hens that eat our corn.
They just stand around looking forlorn.
They said never again would they lay.
As long as our Mistress is gone away.

The cats are catching mice, they don't eat.
And lay them at the door for you a treat.
They sit and beg you will open the door.
So our lives will go on just as before.

MY LIFE

One morning, when I waked up.
I looked out of my door.
I said, "I'm widowed, my kids are gone,
What am I living for?"

The old dog lying by the stoop,
Said, "The cat can catch a mouse,
And I can run and tree a squirrel.
But you're stuck in that old house."

"Grab that old goat by the horns.
Tell the world you're gonna live.
There's lots of things out there to do,
And you've got a lot of cheer to give."

So now I spend a lot of time.
With this lady o'er the way,
I make baskets and we talk.
We laugh and she'll crochet.

No matter what I fix to eat,
What she says makes my heart glad.
"This dinner sure was good today,
It's the best we've ever had."

Ethel Crownover

We drive up to the truck stop,
Lots of days for a bite to eat.
She giggles when I say one day,
A handsome man we'll meet.

With the radio blasting as we drive.
It will melt any weary load.
She says why don't we stop the car
And dance out in the road.

We talk about running away,
Into a far off land.
Never telling our children or anyone,.
And let them find us if they can.

Happiness we've given each other.
And each a reason to live,
It isn't what you get from life that's important
As what it is you can give.

LOOKING BACK

———— ∞ ————

Sausage and biscuit and baked sweet potato,
Wrapped in a paper whose news was months old.
Brings to my mind, a one room school house,
And a rickety bench, where our lessons were told.

Early to bed and up before daylight,
Shivering beside a stove gulping wood.
Its flickering tongues, helped light the kitchen.
How could anyone think this life was good.

Memory to one is oh such a wonder.
Somehow it sorts out the good from the bad.
All the things that were hardships so long ago,
Today are remembered, and make the heart glad.

How fast I would run in the cold frosty morning.
My bare feet would ache as the milking was done.
The hot milk felt good when I missed the bucket.
And back up the hill to the house I would run.

On a path round the mountain, and over the ridge top.
Three miles we walked and thought it was ten.
Those miles I see now, so happy and joyful,
Walking to school and back with my friend.

Ethel Crownover

There's not a day I lived in my childhood,
Though drenched in the rain and dried in the sun.
If I could turn back and live my life over,
Down the same paths I would joyfully run.

A Cry From A Vietnam Vet

Twelve months of my life are gone,
I gave it to the Viet Cong.
I thought, I was doing right,
When I volunteered to fight.
I kissed my Mom and went away,
The sun was shining on that day.
I caught the plane, and waved good-bye,
And prayed she didn't, see me cry.
I felt like a grown up man,
I said I'll do the best I can.
I soon found out, that nothings right,
The little man was forced to fight.
Like me, he couldn't understand,
What I was doing, in this land.
An out is never hard to find,
We smoked pot and blew the mind,
I'm all messed up, I'm ruined for life.
The war goes on, in pain and strife,
How many more must go and see.
There's no such thing, as being free.
The war is planned out, by the rich,
I learned this, while in a ditch.
The leeches and the mud did stink,
And there I had the time to think.

Ethel Crownover

Why did I shoot, and he shoot back,
When all he had, was just a shack.
He died and never did I know why,
He was sent, to fight, and die.
It is a plan, you would call greed,
Kill off the ones, you cannot feed.
My year is up, and I come home,
My sense of value's, now are gone.
The army cares not you're a mess,
They want to teach you how to dress.
And if you cross one little whim,
You're undesirable to them.
All I have now are dreams of fear,
And fright in eyes, of ones so dear.
I'll fool around and sing this song,
And pray my life will not last long.

DEAR DAUGHTER BEWARE

———— ∞ ————

Dear daughter, come here,
Let me give you advice.
On how to choose a man.
Be sure his love is much greater than yours,
Before you give him your hand.

In this world of men,
We have two kind.
There is one that can love with his soul.
Of the other beware, he can never be true.
Like a round rock in a stream, he will roll.

From beginning of time,
There has been two kind,
One's love is much greater than life.
It's up to you, to make the right choice,
To be a slave or a wife.

SERENITY MOUNTAIN

---- ∞ ----

Upon the mountain, wild and high.
I stop to hear the rain crow cry.
The music of a thousand things,
Make me rejoice, the whole world sings.
I hear the buzzing of a bee,
Two squirrels a chattering in a tree.
I stir and everything goes still,
And from the quiet I get a thrill.
So glad am I to hear and see.
The splendor God, has given me.
In sunset glow from yonder hill.
I hear the song of whip-o-will.
How wonderful his joy to share.
As he sings on without a care.
Simple life was meant to be.
God's creatures all but man can see.
He alone from all the rest.
With discontentment in his breast.
Promotes more hatred year by year.
And all the world must live in fear.

OUR SKELETON

———— ∞ ————

You know there is a skeleton,
In every family.
They keep it in their closet.
So no one will ever see.
All families over flow with pride.
And brag of their family name,
And keep tightly locked their closet door.
On their skeleton of shame.
It used to be a foolish child,
They hid from the world.
On a grand child born out of wed lock,
By a poor unfortunate girl.
We got one that won't be found.
Brother-in-law can look and look,
From the attic to the basement,
In every cranny and every nook.
Our skeleton he'll never find.
He'll finally give up and quit.
Our lips are sealed, we'll never tell,
That he married it.

POOR MAN'S BLUES

———————— ∞ ————————

I'm blue and lonesome, lonesome and blue,
But when you got no money, nobody wants you.

This mechanized world done took away my pride.
This mechanized world done took away my pride.
I ain't got enough clothes, in which to hide.

There's lots a pretty women, they all want a man.
There's lots a pretty women, they all want a man.
When you ain't got no money, they turn loose your hand.

I'm traveling to the Southland, the further I go.
I'm traveling to the Southland, the further I go.
There ain't but one difference, I don't walk in the snow.

I got no education, for school I had no time.
I got no education, for school I had no time.
When you got no training, you ain't worth a dime.

I'm singing a sad song, my feet are just like lead,
I'm singing a sad song, my feet are just like lead.
It's a rich man's world, a poor man's better off dead.

MEMORIES

———— ∞ ————

It was about 1928 when this old lady took me down town to the fabu-
lous 'Lowes Theater" in Akron, Ohio to see Al Jolson and Sonny Boy in
person. I guess I was more impressed by the chandeliers and plush
rugs in the lobby, than I was by the fact I was seeing so famous person
as Al Jolson.

SUMMER RAIN

There's nothing like a summer rain.
Mixed with dust, it has a special smell.
Like toadstools in a damp and ferny glade.
So musty sweet as the first raindrops have fell.
The dust is deep between my toes.
The sun is burning hot upon my skin.
There in the west the clouds piled high,
A promise that the rain has come again.
With delight the leaves are dancing in the breeze,
And eagerly await the cool refreshing bath.
The first big drops make puffs of dust,
As they splatter down upon the path.
In sheets the rain comes cross the fields,
Like soldiers marching home from battle won.
Then brushing back the clouds with golden rays,
Peeking at a fresh washed world, the setting sun.

One Day On the Farm

Get up for it will soon be time,
For the cock to crow,
And ere he untucks his head,
You will have plowed a row.

The corns been planted, just two weeks.
Weeds are four weeks ahead.
Get moving, you must battle them,
Till one of you are dead.

You'll soon be galded on the legs,
Salt sweat makes you most blind.
One thing for sure, that you won't have,
Is corns on your behind.

You don't have time but get a drink.
From the water in the creek.
By twelve O'clock the mule and you,
From hunger will be weak.

You don't need a watch to know it's twelve.
The mule will hasten his stride.
He knows when it's time, to eat and drink
Unhitch, hop up, and ride.

Ethel Crownover

You can't spare the time, but take an hour,
For the mule must have his rest.
He'll eat a third of the crop you raise,
And for that, he does his best.

Back to the field, the sun is hot.
The battle is not yet won.
Back and forth, you must follow the mule.
Until the plowing is done.

The sun is sinking in the West,
Most weary are your feet.
Once more the mule, hastens his step,
For he knows it is time to eat.

First you must care for his needs,
When you put him in the barn.
For he who can take it, it's so rewarding,
To get back to the earth and the farm.

YOU CAN'T TELL SIXTEEN FROM SIXTY

This used to be a man's world,
Now the gals have got the floor.
The whole system's upside down,
You can't tell sixteen from sixty any more.

False lashes, wigs, and sexy clothes,
With foundation creams that cover.
You'll find you're swinging a cute chick,
That's older than your mother.

The other night I had a date,
The cutest thing I'd seen.
All the guys were standing round,
With envy turning green.

I asked her where she'd like to go,
And she said anywhere.
And be as reckless as you please,
For I'm on Medicare.

I saw this doll wasting time,
With an old guy, but oh brother.
When I started cutting in,
He said, meet my Grandmother.

Ethel Crownover

Take me back to the good, old days,
When women after thirty.
Had their minds on clothes for kids,
And dishes that were dirty.

THE MIGHTY EAGLE

The Mighty Eagle cannot nest with the Sparrow,
With the broken wing.
She is trapped forever on the ground.
She will pluck his feathers one by one.
Thinking she will also trap him to the earth.

Springtime will come with new feathers.
The mountain top will sparkle in the rising sun.
He sees freedom from the unhappy sparrow.
He cannot live shackled to a mediocre life.
If he stays, freedom will be drained from his blood.

He will become an Eagle with a broken spirit.
He flaps his wings of new feathers, rises on the wind.
Turning into the golden sun in the east, he flies.
Back to the mountain to become again a Mighty Eagle.
Mother Nature will sustain him, Father Time will be gentle.

Unencumbered love is waiting, his fate he will master.
High in the tallest tree, his new feathers sparkle in the sun.
He looks down on the life he has escaped from.
The sparrow with the broken wing will be forgotten.
As he soars high in the sky, back to freedom.

THIS IS LIFE

When I was growing up,
I thought life would be just dandy.
I'd marry to a handsome prince,
And we would live on candy.

An then I wed the farmer's son,
Who thought that married ladies.
Should cook and clean and can up food,
And fill the house with babies.

And he hang up my dancing shoes,
Said he,"You'll need them no more."
They are just too flimsy,
When you scrub up the floor.

You know you married a farmer,
Your duty you cannot shirk.
You must must produce me many sons,
To help me with farm work.

Dear husband you're head of the house,
I'll agree with this by heck.
For the head can do nothing at all,
Without permission from the neck.

TAYLOR, MY GUARDIAN

One of my greatest memories was the summer I was four and Taylor was nine. He swears he don't remember this, but it will forever be embedded in my memory. We lived behind a service station. Back then there were no tanker trucks so gasoline was brought in fifty gallon drums. Taylor pushed me up on an empty drum and I pulled him up. We set up there and struck matches and lit the fumes that were coming from the opening, where the gas was siphoned out. The blaze of fire would swoosh five feet in the air. It really was a lot of fun. Mama and Papa were at work and Taylor was taking care of me.

MAMA'S SOW

———— ∞ ————

When Mama and Papa moved from the little house in Bells Cove on Grandpa's place to across the ridge to farm for Sam Henley, they didn't have to load up the sow to move her. When she saw all the meager house hold goods being hauled off in the wagon, she also saw the hand that fed her in the wagon. She fell in behind the wagon and moved her self.

BLACK MAMA

Which reminds me of when we left Decherd and moved to Deep Woods. We had an old black cat with one eye. Every morning early she would stroll down the walk and go to the stock barn to catch mice. She seemed to be on a schedule and would stroll back just at dusk to get her bowl of milk. That morning as she started down the walk I said, "Black Mama, I'm sorry, but when you come back tonight we will be gone. We are leaving about two o'clock and you will be on your own, like when you came here. I will take your kitten so you won't have any responsibility." She sat and listened; like she understood. every word. At two o'clock when I started down the walk to the car, Black Mama was strolling up to meet me. I picked her up, pitched her in the car and she lived out her days in Deep Woods. Cats that tell time by the sun are scarce.

AN OLD LADY AND HER CAT

One morning about a year after my Husband had passed away, I had a call from a friend asking me to fill in for her, staying with this elderly lady. I had never done anything like that so I said I would give it a try. One day a week wasn't too bad, so I accepted the job. After all, I was alone and had very little to keep my mind and body busy, and was found wondering what good I was to the world in general. Not long after I started on my new adventure, for that was certainly what this turned out to be, my friend got into an argument with her charge and was not allowed to continue. There I was with the whole five days to stay with what every one said, was the most impossible person to get along with in the whole of our community. For quite awhile I kept her entertained with stories of which I had quite a few. I knew what the fellow felt like that had to tell a story to keep from getting his head chopped off, and had to keep it up indifinitely. Then a miracle happened, in the form of a litter of kittens that I had to take with me each day to keep the dog from killing them. I had to feed them on a bottle during the day, since I couldn't take the mother cat too. She loved cats and was so busy helping with them she had nothing to depress her any more. Then the dog got one of them on the week end, then he got the second and then the third. Now I was down to little Tuffy, a brindle and white tom cat. Every day they grew closer to one another, and she was so happy the attention he gave her. He got used to the car and would run and jump in each morning and stretch out on the dashboard. If it rained he would chase the wiper blades across and back with his paw on the windshield. Each morning he would jump out and run to the door and get in her lap. When she crocheted he would take her needles or her thread away and get in her lap so she had to stop every thing and pet him. Sometimes he would sit on the couch beside her and lean back with his head on her shoulder. This pleased her very much and the days went by pleasantly. Every one that knew her would comment on the change in her personality. He loved to stretch out on the coffee table and push everything off in the floor and this would make her laugh. One day she wound up a music box and started it to play beside him on the table. It was turning around and it got his attention and he pushed it away and then pulled it up close and with his teeth turned it off. To her this was one of the smartest things a cat every done. Two years have passed, and each day they sit on the couch together. She will stroke his back and he will purr and reach up and feel of her neck with his paws. Most of the time now he just lays with his head on her lap and sleeps while she does her needle work. When he gets to feeling like being a kitten, he will steal her thimble and chase it around the room. Sometimes I let him spend the night and this makes her happy. I realize she is getting older every day and the time will come when they will both have only the memories of one another. One thing they have together is love, one of the most important things God gave to us when he created the universe. Love makes the world go round. And with it comes happiness, contentment, and a life that is fulfilled. This I learned from an old lady and a cat.

GROVER

—————— ∞ ——————

Mama and Papa moved back to the little house on Grandpa's place when Grover was about six years of age. A little young to walk to Uncle Bill Garner's store on the other side of Providence which would have been at least six miles round trip. Mama told him he could get a nickels worth of suckers for the three of us. For a child so young, it was a long tiresome trip and I guess he did get hungry, for back in them days, I guess we were hungry all the time. When he got home with the candy, he had sucked them all so thin you could have read the newspaper through them.

In 1930 when we moved from the city back into Bells Cove, we had to walk across the ridge of the mountain to the one room school in Providence. Just out of the city where we spent each Saturday in the movies watching the cowboys and Indians, I guess Taylor and I were pretty gullible so when Grover drove an arrowhead into a cedar tree on the path we had to walk and told us an Indian had shot at him, of course we believed him.

Another time he ran off and left me alone about half way across the ridge coming from school. When I finally caught up with him, he was lying stretched out in the path with a huge stick by his head like some-one had knocked him out. I noticed he had placed his cap under his head, so I grabbed up the stick and said I think he is still breathing, so I'll just finish him off. He came up from there in a hurry, and we went on together.

One night Grover and our cousin Paul were coming across the ridge to home when they heard this fellow whistling that had been up in the cove courting a girl. They stepped off the path behind trees and as he passed Grover stepped behind him and put his arms around him and pulled him up against his body. His head dropped on Grover's shoulder and he started so they said, to bleat like a sheep. They thought they had scared him to death.

Another time Grover and Paul got sheets and waited on a group of folks that had walked to the cove to a party. Grover wrapped up in one sheet and got Paul on his shoulders and then he wrapped up in another sheet. They stood behind a tree and stepped out behind the last one to pass by. The path is narrow and one had to walk single file. They noticed that tall white thing behind them so they started walking faster. The faster they went, the faster the thing behind them would go. They started to run and Grover had no way to see, but he started to run also, with Paul trying to steer him in the dark, since the moon had gone behind a cloud. Grover ran off in a ravine about six foot deep and almost killed the both of them.

GROVER'S WORST TRICK

Sometime back in the early thirties, my brother Grover and our cousin Albert Edwards were crossing the ridge that separated Bells Cove from Providence. It was an early fall day and cool enough for a jacket, but up in the day, it got too hot for one. John Rice had gone ahead of them and got a little warm and had pulled off his coat and hung it on a bush beside the path with his cap. When my brother and cousin came along and found them, they decided to make a dummy by stuffing the coat with leaves. About the time they got their dummy made, Grover's nose began to bleed, so he let it bleed on a big stick and let some drop on the cap. He laid the stick by the head of his creation and then piled leaves like the rest of the body was under the leaves. A man and his wife back further in the head of the cove had been having trouble and she had left him and the four kids and returned to where she had come from. My step grandmother was way up in years, but she had taken the youngest girl in, no doubt to have someone to wait on her. That morning she decided to go to Providence and the little girl was with her when she came upon my brothers work of art lying by the side of the path. Granny wore her dresses down to her ankles and high top shoes, since she hadn't seen the latest fashions from Paris. She turned back towards the cove yanking her skirts up over her knees and screaming every breath that this man had killed his wife. The girl right behind her scared to death that her mother was lying dead beside the path. Way up in the cove, Grandpa heard her coming and grabbed his old pistol and met her at the foot of the hill, where they said she cleared the rail fence on the way to the house. Grandpa took off fast as he could go to see what had scared the old lady to put so much life back in her. He had also gone over that rail fence with just one leap and talk about mad when he found the cause of all the trouble, he put up a five hundred dollar reward for information on who had done so dastardly a deed. Since everyone knew he didn't have that much money, no one ever told him who the culprit was.

GRANDFATHER'S TALES

To have known, Christopher Columbus Partin was in itself one of the greatest experiences of ones life. True or not he could entertain us for hours with his stories, and I believed them all, however, I was skeptical of the one about the cats. As a young man, he had a long red beard, almost to his waist. I have a picture of him with his second wife. It was taken on the farm where I grew up, by an old log house that I can remember. My oldest brother, Grover went to house keeping there when he married. Mama said Grandpa C.C., as we called him, used to wear galluses made from strips of hickory bark and fastened them to his pants with nails. I let Alice take the picture to make a copy. She sent me the copy. It had Papa, Aunt Bessie, Pat as a baby in his mother's arms. Grandpa and Papa were sitting down. The others were standing. Evidently they had just two chairs.

THE SPELL

───── ∞ ─────

One morning when Grandpa C.C. looked out the door, his house was surrounded by cats all over the rail fence and peeping through the cracks of the lower rails. He ran out and grabbed up a green walnut and knocked one in the head killing it dead. About this same time an old woman living across the field fell dead. The cats disappeared, and Grandpa said he had broke the spell this witch had over the cats and the dead cat was really her.

THE COVIL WAR SAGA

———— ∞ ————

One of his greatest tales was about the Civil War. His Father refused to become involved on either side. As you know from history Tennessee was divided in their feelings. Brothers served on both sides. As for Great-Grandfather Jack, he wasn't mad at any one. All he had was a little homestead in Roark's cove which he haphazardly farmed at his own pace. The only slave he had was his two thirds Cherokee wife who was the strength of the family. When the pressure got more than they could handle for him to take sides they buried all their breakable goods and left for Indiana in an ox drawn wagon behind the Union lines. No doubt the wife had the husband buried in the straw when they encountered either side of the conflict. Grandpa told of how he walked to Indiana and back when a mere boy. Since they had a new baby every two or three years the proof is in the birth records. His sister, Unity, was born in Indiana and the other children before her and after were born in Tennessee. The name in itself shows they believed in the Unity of this country. Great-Grandmother was very American in choosing her children's names, America, Tennessee, Caroline were some of his sisters and a brother George from the first President. They came into Tennessee through the Carolinas so they kept a record by the children's names. I have in my possession a hand blown lamp that was one of the items buried when they drove away from the little homestead, where they returned after the war was over.

THE DUCK HUNT

———— ∞ ————

This one he told about a duck hunt; Down behind the old farm house where Grandpa lived when a boy, was a pond. One morning he walked down with the old muzzle loader to get duck for dinner. Hiding behind an old chestnut rail fence, he saw two ducks swimming together. Thinking if he waited until he could get them in line, he could get both with one shot, he waited patiently. He knew he couldn't shoot one, reload, and fire again before the other duck could rise and fly away. Finally, he gave up and fired and killed one. The other duck came up off the water, got airborne, and started flying away. It made a turn, to get in the wind current, and was coming straight toward where Grandpa stood behind the rail fence. Just as it was to pass overhead, Grandpa C.C. said he jumped straight up and grabbed it by the neck.

THE FUNERAL AND THE WEDDING

This one we always took with a grain of salt. I do know long years ago, if one wanted to get married all you needed was a traveling preacher to perform the ceremony. You didn't have to pay the state for a privilege given by the Master above. Grandpa had a cousin, a fairly young man, whose wife passed away. At the burying, it took, three of the neighbor men to restrain him from jumping in the open grave, to go with his beloved wife. After the funeral was over while traveling home, he got married. He said he remembered, he couldn't make biscuits.

THE STORY OF THE BEAR

———— ∞ ————

And next comes the story of the Bear. One time Roark's Cove was invaded by a bear, so my Grandpa told us. The dogs had the bear treed and were really having a knock down, drag out fight. When Grandpa saw the dogs were losing, he went to help. In his own words he said , "I jumped on that Bear and fit it for hours." He told us he pulled enough fur out of that bear's hide to furnish Roark's Cove School with chalk erasers for a whole year. He never did tell us what happened to the be r.

GRANDPA C.C.'S ADVICE

Grandpa C.C. was really a sharp old bird. We were truly fascinated by him. We paid attention to his advice; since he told it in a way that was not easily forgotten. He said to never, never, date a boy you wouldn't consider for a husband. His policy was; "You could keep an old hound dog around long enough to learn to love it.

Another bit of advice was; "When a man was chasing a woman, it was liken to a dog, chasing a rabbit. As long as that rabbit stayed ahead, the dog just kept after it. All the fun was over ,when the rabbit gave up the chase.

GRANDPA'S COUSIN COLE YOUNGER

Grandpa always claimed Cole Younger was a cousin of his. Whether or not there was any truth to this story, we never knew. We never did look into this claim, since we didn't want to hurt Grandpa's feelings by letting him think we doubted his truthfulness. I for one was quite fascinated by this story and have shared it along with many others told by this fascinating old guy. Anyway, he said that his cousin, Cole Younger, rode with Jesse James on many a train robbery. Once while robbing a train, he spied this little old lady with a new pair of hightop shoes on, like they wore in those days. He just knew they would fit his wife, so he actually took them off her feet. When she tried to fight him for her shoes; he slapped her face with the soles.

GRANDPA'S YOUNGER DAY SHENANIGANS

Sometimes Grandpa would tell us stories of when he was a young man, before he married. And some were a little bit off color, as one might have thought in those days before T.V. One night he joined a bunch of boys that planned to go play peeping Tom at this girls house. She was having girls sleep over. Back in those days the houses mostly didn't have glass windows. Just wooden shutters you closed in bad weather. In hot weather they stayed open day and night, dogs, cats and chickens wandered in and out at will. That was the day of kerosene lamps, so at best the boys couldn't see much as the girls undressed for bed. But to get back to C.C. crouching under one such window with the boys. He said they were all getting an eyeful of the girls undressing for bed when a girl, with a well endowed bosom, got real close to the window. He jumped up, grabbed her by one of them and she screamed. Boy he hit that mountain running with the rest of the boys right behind him. The old man just got off one shot, you see, he was shooting a muzzle loader.

When my Papa was a young man, he went to Chapman's Chapel to church, after having been out drinking the night before. Evidently he had not fully sobered up. It was in the summer time and he went in and stuck his feet up on the stove and said, "Sing the last song in the book while I warm my toes," and kicked the stove over. This is how he wound up in Texas at his Aunt Amy Coker's. He had to leave Tennessee on the run. This happened many, many years ago, but even today, you will hear occasionally someone say, "Sing the last song in the book, while I warm my toes." I guess when he kicked the stove over in the church, it made a lasting impression.

GREAT-GRANDPA JACK

———— ∞ ————

I guess from all the tales I've heard about my Papa's family; they were all just a little off the beaten path, so to speak. Great-Grandpa was quite a creature of habit. He always wore his hat. The first thing he put on every morning was his hat, that had been resting under the head of his bed overnight, and the last thing to be removed, when he lay down to rest. For no other reason did he remove that hat, except to sleep. Once when he had to go to court, the judge asked him to remove his hat. He refused. The judge said, " Mr. Partin, if you don't remove your hat, I will have to fine you ten dollars for contempt of court. " Great-Grandpa Jack walked up and laid ten dollars down in front of the judge. Then the judge asked him again to remove his hat. Great-Grandpa Jack said," Judge, I have just paid you ten dollars to wear my hat, and I'm gonna wear it."

Besides wearing his hat, Great-Grandpa Jack always wore his best clothes every day and walked around like a Southern Gentleman. God only knows how he made a living, but living back then was simple. A few cows and chickens could keep a family going, especially if you had a thrifty wife that made a garden, canned and stored away every thing imaginable for winter. But on this one occasion, he invited the preacher home to dinner without getting permission from his wife. That was in the days before Women's Lib, when women were in complete control of the household. All she had cooked was turnip greens and cornbread. Great-Grandpa Jack passed the greens to the preacher and learned, he didn't eat them. Great-Grandpa Jack jumped up, ran out the door and wrung the head off a frying chicken. After all, all preachers love fried chicken.

GREAT-GRANDMA MARY ANNE

Once when Great-Grandma MaryAnne was way along in years , she took to her sick bed as they said back in those days, and had to be set up with at night. The widow from next door started coming over to set the night with Great-Grandpa Jack and help with the care of his wife. It didn't take long for Grandpa Jack to start thinking of the future as Grandma didn't seem to be getting any better. So he started discussing the future with the widow, from next door. This led to their plans to marry, just as soon as they had Great-Grandma Mary Anne tucked away beneath the sod. But she didn't die, and the widow later told of her plans to marry Great-Grandma's husband. Great-Grandma Mary Anne lived to bury them both. They had given her an incentive to live.

GREAT GRANDMA MARY ANNE'S ADVICE

Great-Grandmother was a very intelligent lady and her bits of advice have been handed down through the generations to females of the family. Her thinking on sex education was very simple and to the point; "Any one can take care of a little patch of hair one can cover with one hand". And another famous quote was; "Don't let him get to the bait, till you get his foot in the trap.

UNCLE JOE

Uncle Joe was the last to be born. Great-Grandmother was fifty or more when he came along. If there ever was a character in this world it was Papa's Uncle Joe. One time at Christmas, Papa was a little fellow living with his Grandparents since his Mother had died when he was just a child. He wanted a rocking horse from Santa Claus and talked about it day and night. All he wanted was this horse. Christmas morning he ran down the stairs to find Uncle Joe standing beside this little horse laying on its side. He said to Papa, I'm sorry about your rocking horse but he messed on the floor and I just had to shoot him. Poor Papa fell down to the floor crying.

When Uncle Joe got to be a young man, taking care of his aging parents and and the house hold chores and all the cooking was placed on his shoulders. He had the milking and churning along with all the other chores his aging parents didn't feel like doing. The worst thing in the world to deal with is one of them old cedar churns, with a lid that fit on top, and no way to make it hold on when churning. They seemed to delight in jumping off the churn. Uncle Joe solved this problem by placing the churn outside the kitchen door and setting his feet on the lid to hold it steady.

GRANNY MARTHA

I guess you might say both sides of my family had strange characters in it. This must be the reason I've always marched to a different drummer than the average person. My Granny, on my Mama's side of the family, lived out on the other side of Monteagle Mountain, on a bluff; sort a like where I live today. First time I ever saw her, I was ten and I thought she was over a hundred at that time. We went out one time to see about her, when it had come a big snow, since she lived alone. She had a fire in the fireplace that I could have scooped up in one hand. On the fire she had this little can cooking something. Since this was Depression Days I was interested in what was on a cooking. When I asked ,she said it was walnut kernels she was rendering out to get the grease to fry an egg. The Grandson had not brought her groceries and she was out of lard, so she said. When I asked why she didn't just boil the egg ; which to me was the most logical thing to do, she snapped at me like a snapping turtle, "Because I wanted a fried one".

And there was this other time, when a cousin and her parents went out to see the old lady. This was what was known as the pocket, and lots of unsavory characters lived out there. Granny had gone to milk and when she came to the house with an empty bucket she said the cow had got in some one's still and was so drunk she wouldn't let her milk, because she was dog drunk.

Granny was less than five feet in height and three years before she died Mama moved her down to the farm, to take care of her. I'll always remember what she said when she learned she was not to return to her little house in the pocket. She said she would make Mama regret, till the day she died, that she had moved her. When she was ninety-four years of age, I saw Granny dance in her sock feet and say, "Watch me do the Buck and Wing."

Granny was a tobacco chewer and never had the attention of a doctor, till it was necessary to have one pronounce her dead. She had twelve children . She even pulled her own teeth down to one tooth in front, that she used to hook into a chicken leg and rip all the meat off. She said ," I owe my long life to clean living, staying away from them doctors, and tending to my own business."

About the Author

————— ∞ —————

I grew up on a farm during the depression days. We were self support-
ing and I remember my childhood as the most wonderful time of my
life. We attended a one room school 2 1/2 miles away where on a path
we walked from the Cove across a ridge. My grandfather was a great
teller of tales and never tired repeating amazing stores of days of his
growing up. I started writing them down and have repeated them to
schools, clubs and as an after dinner speaker.

My education did not exceed the twelfth grade and my graduation
class had less than fifty students. Again I walked 2 1/2 miles to catch a
bus built on the bed of a hay truck. I remember those first days scared to
death of being in what I thought was all the people on earth. Only one
of the three that finished the 8th grade with me went on to high school
and we clung together like two scared rabbits. It was there the world
opened up to me in our little library and I was determined one day to
see all those wonderful places.

I have traveled through all of the states except Alaska and hopefully I
will go there one day. Also through part of Canada and ten countries in
Europe. Although English was one of my best subjects you will find I
speak the language of the Tennessee backwoods.

My poetry is about my life, my friend's lives and the mountains I love
so much in the South Eastern part of Tennessee. My poetry, so different
from what you may have read, will bring joy and tears to the elderly, and
to the young, laughter and wonder of what my world was all about.